A BESTIARY

COMPILED BY RICHARD WILBUR

ILLUSTRATED BY ALEXANDER CALDER

Pantheon Books

NEW YORK

Grateful acknowledgment is made to the following for the use of material quoted: Appleton-Century-Crofts, Inc., "The Flower-Fed Buffaloes" from *Going-to-the-Stars* by Vachel Lindsay. Copyright, 1926, D. Appleton & Company. Reprinted by permission of the publishers Appleton-Century-Crofts, Inc. Barnes and Noble. Inc., passage from *Beasts and Saints*, translated by Helen Waddell. Botteghe Oscure, "Beasts," by Richard Wilbur. Clarendon Press, passage from Plato's *Phaedrus*, translated by Benjamin Jowett. Dodd, Mead and Company, Inc., passage from *Bramble-bees and Others* by J. Henri Fabre. Copyright 1915 by Dodd, Mead and Company. Doubleday and Company, Inc., passage from *Seven Pillars of Wisdom*, by T. E. Lawrence. Copyright 1926, 1935 by Doubleday and Company, Inc. E.P. Dutton and Company, Inc., passage from *Nature in Downland* and *Far Away and Long Ago*, by W. H. Hudson; passage from *The Little Flowers* of *St. Francis*, translated by Thomas Okey. Harcourt, Brace and Company, Inc., for "Death of a Toad" from *Ceremony and Other Poems*, by Richard Wilbur. Harper and Brothers, passage from *The Human Comedy*, by James Harvey Robinson. Houghton Mifflin Company, passage from "The Fish," from *North and South*, by Elizabeth Bishop. Harold Ober Associates, passage from "I Want to Know Why" from *The Triumph of the Egg*, by Sherwood Anderson. Copyright, 1921, by Eleanor Anderson. The Macmillan Company, "The Centaurs" from *Collected Poems of James Stephens;* passage from the *Diary* of the Rev. James Kilvert, edited by William Plomer; "Rigorists" from *What Are Years*, by Marianne Moore; "Sheep" from *Valhalla and Other Poems*, by Robert Francis. Manchester University Press, passage from *Animals for Show and Pleasure in Ancient Rome*, by George Jennison. McGraw-Hill Book Company, passage from *Boswell on the Grand Tour: Germany and Switzerland*, edited by F. A. Pottle. Mercure de France, "A Prayer to Go to Paradise with the Donkeys," translated by Richard Wilbur from *Elégies et autres vers*, by Francis Jammes. New Directions, translation by Dudley Fitts of the poem by Tymnes from *100 Poems from the Palatine Anthology*. W. W. Norton Company, Inc., passage from *The Revolt of the Masses*, by José Ortega y Gasset. Oxford University Press, Inc., "S. Thomae Aquinatis" and "Repeat that, Repeat," from *Poems of Gerard Manley Hopkins;* "Concord Cats" from *Undercliff*, by Richard Eberhart. Princeton University Press, passage from the *Memoirs* of Usāmah ibn-Munqidh, translated by Philip K. Hitti. G. P. Putnam's Sons, passage from Oppian's "Cynegetica" in *Oppian*, etc., translated by A. W. Mair. Random House, passage from *The Prince*, by Niccolò Machiavelli, translated by Luigi Ricci, translation revised by E. R. P. Vincent; passage from "The Bear" from *Go Down, Moses*, by William Faulkner; passage from the introduction by William Butler Yeats to *Irish Fairy and Folk Tales*. Schocken Books, Inc., passage from Franz Kafka's *Parables*, translated by Clement Greenberg and others. Charles Scribner's Sons, passage from *Falconry*, by W. J. Russell; passage from *The Criminal*, by Havelock Ellis. University of Chicago Press, passage from Homer's *Iliad*, translated by Richard Lattimore, reprinted by permission of The University of Chicago Press. Copyright, 1951, by The University of Chicago.

Originally published in the United States by Pantheon Books in 1955 in a signed, limited edition designed by Joseph Blumenthal at The Spiral Press.

ISBN: 0-679-42875-5

Manufactured in the United States of America
Pantheon Books Edition 1993
9 8 7 6 5 4 3 2 1

THE
CONTENTS

BEASTS

Beasts in their major freedom
Slumber in peace tonight. The gull on his ledge
Dreams in the guts of himself the moon-plucked waves below,
And the sunfish leans on a stone, slept
By the lyric water;

In which the spotless feet
Of deer make dulcet splashes, and to which
The ripped mouse, safe in the owl's talon, cries
Concordance. Here there is no such harm
And no such darkness

As the selfsame moon observes
Where, warped in window-glass, it sponsors now
The werewolf's painful change. Turning his head away
On the sweaty bolster, he tries to remember
The mood of manhood

But lies at last, as always,
Letting it happen, the fierce fur soft to his face,
Hearing with sharper ears the wind's exciting minors,
The leaves' panic, and the degradation
Of the heavy streams.

Meantime, at high windows
Far from thicket and pad-fall, suitors of excellence
Sigh and turn from their work to construe again the painful
Beauty of heaven, the lucid moon
And the risen hunter,

Making such dreams for men
As told will break their hearts as always, bringing
Monsters into the city, crows on the public statues,
Navies fed to the fish in the dark
Unbridled waters.

R. W.

THE FROG

UPON THE FROG

The frog by nature is both damp and cold,
Her mouth is large, her belly much will hold;
She sits somewhat ascending, loves to be
Croaking in gardens, though unpleasantly.

COMPARISON

The hypocrite is like unto this frog,
As like as is the puppy to the dog.
He is of nature cold, his mouth is wide
To prate, and at true goodness to deride.
He mounts his head as if he was above
The world, when yet 'tis that which has his love.
And though he seeks in churches for to croak,
He neither loveth Jesus nor his yoke.

John Bunyan, *Divine Emblems*

In the spring of the year when the birds sing, the frogs and toads also croak. So at the same time that the Saints sing God's praises, hypocrites sing also, but the voice is as different in God's ear as the sweet singing of birds and the croaking of toads and frogs.

Jonathan Edwards, Images or Shadows

SAINT BENNO AND THE FROG

It was often the habit of the man of God to go about the fields in meditation and prayer: and once as he passed by a certain marsh, a talkative frog was croaking in its slimy waters: and lest it should disturb his contemplation, he bade it be a Seraphian, inasmuch as all the frogs in Seraphus are mute. But when he had gone on a little way, he called to mind the saying in Daniel: *"O ye whales and all that move in the waters, bless ye the Lord. O all ye beasts and cattle, bless ye the Lord."* And fearing lest the singing of the frogs might perchance be more agreeable to God than his own praying, he again issued his command to them, that they should praise God in their accustomed fashion: and soon the air and the fields were vehement with their conversation.

Jerome Emser, Life of St. Benno

In Cyrene, the frogs were formerly dumb, and this species still exists, although croaking ones were carried over there from the continent. At the present day, even, the frogs in the island of Seraphus are dumb; but when they are carried to other places, they croak. . . .

Pliny, Natural History

A beautiful green frog inhabits the grassy, marshy shores of these large rivers. They are very numerous, and their noise exactly resembles the barking of little dogs, or the yelping of puppies: these likewise make a great clamour, but as their notes are fine, and uttered in chorus, by separate bands or communities, far and near, rising and falling with the gentle breezes, it affords a pleasing kind of music.

William Bartram, Travels

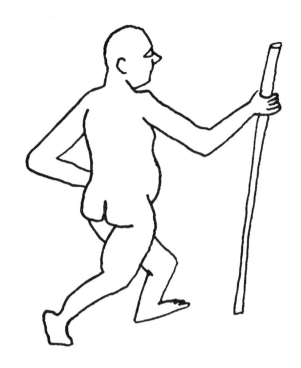

THE DOG

Theseus.   My hounds are bred out of the Spartan kind,
    So flew'd, so sanded; and their heads are hung
    With ears that sweep away the morning dew;
    Crook-knee'd, and dew-lapt like Thessalian Bulls;
    Slow in pursuit, but match'd in mouth like bells,
    Each under each. A cry more tuneable
    Was never holla'd to, nor cheer'd with horn,
    In Crete, in Sparta, nor in Thessaly:
    Judge, when you hear.

William Shakespeare, *A Midsummer Night's Dream*

The dog is the most complete, the most remarkable, and the most useful conquest ever made by man. Every species has become our property; each individual is altogether devoted to his master, assumes his manners, knows and defends his property, and remains attached to him until death: and all this proceeds neither from want nor constraint, but solely from true gratitude and real friendship. The swiftness, the strength, and the scent of the dog, have created for man a powerful ally against other animals, and were perhaps necessary to the establishment of society. He is the only animal who has followed man through every region of the earth.

Baron Cuvier, *The Animal Kingdom*

He is the filthiest of the domestic animals in his person and the nastiest in his habits. For this he makes up in a servile, fawning attitude towards his master, and a readiness to inflict damage and discomfort on all else. The dog, then, commends itself to our favour by affording play to our propensity for mastery, and as he is also an item of expense, and commonly serves no industrial purpose, he holds a well-assured place in men's regard as a thing of good repute. The dog is at the same time associated in our imagination with the chase—a meritorious employment and an expression of the honourable predatory impulse.

Thorstein Veblen, *Theory of the Leisure Class*

EPITAPH OF A MALTESE WATCH-DOG

Beneath me (says the stone) lies the white dog from Melita,
The faithful sentinel of Eumelos' house:

living,

His name was Bully Boy: but now, in death,
His barking is hushed in the empty ways of night.

Tymnes

He heard the changed note in the hounds' uproar and two hundred yards ahead he saw them. The bear had turned. He saw Lion drive in without pausing and saw the bear strike him aside and lunge into the yelling hounds and kill one of them almost in its tracks and whirl and run again. Then they were in a streaming tide of dogs. He heard Major de Spain and Tennie's Jim shouting and the pistol sound of Tennie's Jim's leather thong as he tried to turn them. Then he and Sam Fathers were riding alone. One of the hounds had kept on with Lion though. He recognized its voice. It was the young hound which even a year ago had had no judgment and which, by the lights of the other hounds anyway, still had none. *Maybe that's what courage is,* he thought.

William Faulkner, *The Bear*

THE CENTAURS

Playing upon the hill three centaurs were!
They lifted each a hoof! They stared at me
And stamped the dust!

They stamped the dust! They snuffed upon the air!
And all their movements had the fierce glee
Of power, and pride, and lust!

Of power and pride and lust! Then, with a shout,
They tossed their heads, and wheeled, and galloped round,
In furious brotherhood!

In furious brotherhood! Around, about,
They charged, they swerved, they leaped! Then, bound on bound,
They raced into the wood!

James Stephens

You must know, then, that there are two methods of fighting, the one by law, the other by force: the first method is that of men, the second of beasts; but as the first method is often insufficient, one must have recourse to the second. It is therefore necessary for a prince to know well how to use both the beast and the man. This was covertly taught to rulers by ancient writers, who relate how Achilles and many others of those ancient princes were given to Chiron the centaur to be brought up and educated under his discipline. The parable of this semi-animal, semi-human teacher is meant to indicate that a prince must know how to use both natures, and that the one without the other is not durable.

Niccoló Machiavelli, The Prince

Learne, that this *halfe-a man* and *halfe-a horse,*
Is ancient *Hieroglyphicke,* teaching thee,
That, *wisedome* should be joyn'd with outward *force,*
If prosperous, we desire our workes to be.
His *Upper-part,* the shape of *Man,* doth beare,
To teach, that, *Reason* must become our guide.
The *hinder-parts,* a *Horses* Members are;
To shew, that we must, also, *strength* provide . . .

George Wither, Emblemes

THE APE

Though he endeavour all he can
An *Ape* will never be a *Man*.
George Wither, *Emblemes*

But having sailed three daies by fierie Rivers, we arrived in a Gulfe called Notuceras, that is, the South horne: in the inner part thereof there was a little Iland . . . which had a Lake in it, and in that there was another Iland full of Savage men, but the women were more; they had their bodies all over haire, and of our Interpreters they were called Gorgones: we pursued the men but could take none, for they fled into precipices and defended themselves with stones; but we tooke three of the women, which did nothing but bite and scratch those that led them, and would not follow them. Therefore they killed them, and flead them, and brought their skins to Carthage. . . .

Hanno, *Periplus*

8

The question is this: Is man an ape or an angel? My lord, I am on the side of the angels. I repudiate with indignation and abhorrence the contrary view, which is, I believe, foreign to the conscience of humanity.

Benjamin Disraeli, *Speech to the Oxford Diocesan Society*

Only by comprehending our monkey nature can we have any idea as to why man has surpassed the other animals. Monkeys are dominated by a master passion for monkeying — by an avid curiosity. Man possessed this to a greater degree than the other monkeys, and he has, therefore, outdistanced his simian relatives.

James Harvey Robinson, *The Human Comedy*

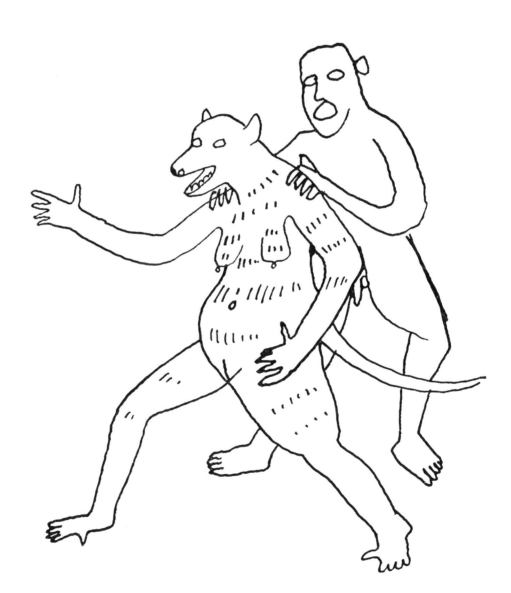

I saw in Southwark, at St. Margaret's fair, monkeys and apes dance, and do other feats of activity, on the high rope; they were gallantly clad *à la mode*, went upright, saluted the company bowing and pulling off their hats, they saluted one another with as good a grace, as if instructed by a dancing-master; they turned heels over head with a basket having eggs in it, without breaking any; also, with lighted candles in their hands, and on their heads, without extinguishing them, and with vessels of water without spilling a drop.

John Evelyn, *Diary*

Mowgli had never seen an Indian city before, and though this was almost a heap of ruins it seemed very wonderful and splendid. Some king had built it long ago on a little hill. . . . The monkeys called the place their city, and pretended to despise the Jungle People because they lived in the forest. And yet they never knew what the buildings were made for nor how to use them. They would sit in circles on the hall of the king's council-chamber, and scratch for fleas and pretend to be men; or they would run in and out of the roofless houses and collect pieces of plaster and old bricks in a corner, and forget where they had hidden them, and fight and cry in scuffling crowds, and then break off to play up and down the terraces of the king's garden, where they would shake the rose-trees and the oranges in sport to see the fruit and flowers fall. They explored all the passages and dark tunnels in the palace and the hundreds of little dark rooms; but they never remembered what they had seen and what they had not, and so drifted about in ones and twos or crowds, telling one another that they were doing as men did. They drank at the tanks and made the water all muddy, and then they fought over it, and then they would all rush together in mobs and shout: "There are none in the jungle so wise and good and clever and strong and gentle as the Bandar-log."

Rudyard Kipling, *The Jungle Book*

THE HORSE

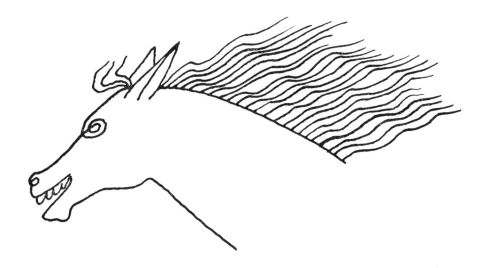

Hast thou given the horse strength? hast thou clothed his
    neck with thunder?
Canst thou make him afraid as a grasshopper? the glory of
    his nostrils is terrible.
He paweth in the valley, and rejoiceth in his strength: he
    goeth on to meet the armed men.
He mocketh at fear, and is not affrighted; neither turneth
    he back from the sword.
The quiver rattleth against him, the glittering spear and
    the shield.
He swalloweth the ground with fierceness and rage: neither
    believeth he that it is the sound of the trumpet.
He saith among the trumpets, Ha, ha; and he smelleth the battle
    afar off, the thunder of the captains, and the shouting.

Job

Honor lives in the manes of horses.
                                    Arab proverb

A generous creature a horse is, sensible in some sort of honor, made most handsome by (that which deforms man most) pride.
                                    Thomas Fuller, *History of the Worthies*

Dauphin. I will not change my horse with any that treads but on four pasterns. *Ça, ha!* He bounds from the earth as if his entrails were hairs: *le cheval volant,* the Pegasus, *qui a les narines de feu!* When I bestride him, I soar, I am a hawk: he trots the air; the earth sings when he touches it; the basest horn of his hoof is more musical than the pipe of Hermes.
                                    William Shakespeare, *Henry V*

If you've never been crazy about thoroughbreds it's because you've never been around where they are much and don't know any better. They're beautiful. There isn't anything so lovely and clean and full of spunk and honest and everything as some race horses. . . .

It brings a lump into my throat when a horse runs. I don't mean all horses but some. I can pick them nearly every time. It's in my blood like in the blood of race-track niggers and trainers. Even when they just go slop-jogging along with a little nigger on their backs I can tell a winner. If my throat hurts and it's hard for me to swallow, that's him. He'll run like Sam Hill when you let him out. If he don't win every time it'll be a wonder and because they've got him in a pocket behind another or he was pulled or got off bad at the post or something. If I wanted to be a gambler like Henry Rieback's father I could get rich. I know I could and Henry says so too. All I would have to do is to wait 'till that hurt comes when I see a horse and then bet every cent.
                                    Sherwood Anderson, *I Want to Know Why*

THE CAMEL

The *Camell* is of nature flexible,
For when a burden on his backe is bound,
To ease the labourer, he is knowne most gentle,
For why he kneeleth downe upon the ground:
  Suffering the man to put it off or on,
  As it seemes best in his discretion.

Robert Chester, *Love's Martyr*

I strained my ears. . . . A pause, while the camel-riders drew up: and then the soggy tapping of canes on the thick of the beasts' necks to make them kneel.

They knelt without a noise: and I timed it in my memory: first the hesitation, as the camels, looking down, felt the soil with one foot for a soft place; then the muffled thud and the sudden loosening of breath as they dropped on their fore-legs, since this party had come far and were tired; then the shuffle as the hind legs were folded in, and the rocking as they tossed from side to side thrusting outward with their knees to bury them in the cooler subsoil below the burning flints, while the riders, with a quick soft patter of bare feet, like birds over the ground, were led off tacitly either to the coffee hearth or to Abdulla's tent, according to their business. The camels would rest there, uneasily switching their tails across the shingle till their masters were free and looked to their stabling.

T. E. Lawrence, *Seven Pillars of Wisdom*

A CAMEL AT FIRST SIGHT

Upon the first sight of a camel, all people ran away from't, in amazement at so monstrous a bulk. Upon the second sight, finding that it did them no hurt, they took heart upon't, went up to't, and view'd it. But when they came, upon further experience, to take notice, how stupid a beast it was, they ty'd it up, bridled it, loaded it with packs and burdens; set boys upon the back on't, and treated it with the last degree of contempt.

THE MORAL

Novelty surprises us, and we have naturally a horror for uncouth misshapen monsters; but 'tis our ignorance that staggers us, for upon custom and experience, all these buggs grow familiar, and easy to us.

Aesop, according to Sir Roger L'Estrange

14

The *Camel* is an animal sufficiently well known; in Chaldean he is called *Civoi;* in Greek *Iphim.* If his blood be poured into the skin of a *tarantula*, or *stellion*, while the stars are shining, one will think to see a giant, whose head will seem to touch the heavens. *Hermes* asserts that he has performed this experiment personally. Should anyone by chance eat of the camel, he will shortly afterward become mad: & if one lights a lamp which has previously been rubbed with camel-blood, it will appear that all present have the heads of *camels*; provided, however, that there are no other lighted lamps in the room.

Secrets of Albertus Magnus

THE MOUSE

A MOUSE'S NEST

I found a ball of grass among the hay
And progged it as I passed and went away;
And when I looked I fancied something stirred,
And turned agen and hoped to catch the bird —
When out an old mouse bolted in the wheats
With all her young ones hanging at her teats;
She looked so odd and so grotesque to me,
I ran and wondered what the thing could be,
And pushed the knapweed bunches where I stood;
Then the mouse hurried from the craking brood.
The young ones squeaked, and as I went away
She found her nest agen among the hay.
The water o'er the pebbles scarce could run
And broad old cesspools glittered in the sun.

John Clare

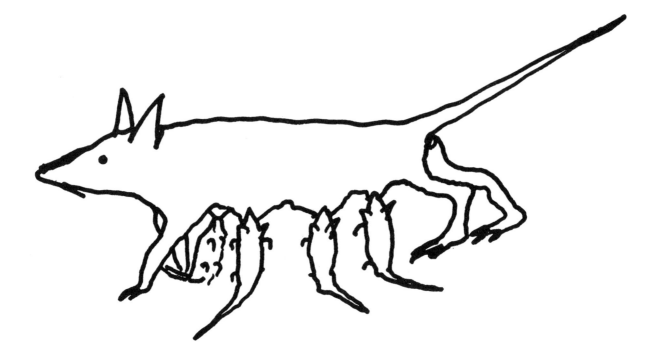

The mice which haunted my house were not the common ones, which are said to have been introduced into the country, but a wild native kind not found in the village. I sent one to a distinguished naturalist, and it interested him much. When I was building, one of these had its nest underneath the house, and before I had laid the second floor, and swept out the shavings, would come out regularly at lunch time and pick up the crumbs at my feet. It probably had never seen a man before; and it soon became quite familiar, and would run over my shoes and up my clothes. It could readily ascend the sides of the room by short impulses, like a squirrel, which it resembled in its motions. At length, as I leaned with my elbow on the bench one day, it ran up my clothes, and along my sleeve, and round and round the paper which held my dinner, while I kept the latter close, and dodged and played at bo-peep with it; and when at last I held still a piece of cheese between my thumb and finger, it came and nibbled it, sitting in my hand, and afterward cleaned its face and paws, like a fly, and walked away.

H. D. Thoreau, *Walden*

One of the characteristics of the leopard is that in case it wounds a man and a mouse urinates on the wound, the man dies. It is very difficult to keep the mouse away from one wounded by a leopard. In fact, they sometimes go so far as to fix a bed for him in the midst of water and tie cats all around him for fear of the mice.

Usāmah ibn-Munqidh, *Memoirs*

THE FLY

Little Fly,
Thy summer's play
My thoughtless hand
Has brush'd away.

Am I not
A fly like thee?
Or art not thou
A man like me?

For I dance,
And drink, & sing,
Till some blind hand
Shall brush my wing.

If thought is life
And strength & breath,
And the want
Of thought is death;

Then am I
A happy fly,
If I live
Or if I die.

William Blake

To return to the insects of the downs. Of these flies thrust themselves most on our attention; it is, in fact, impossible to overlook creatures that conduct themselves in so wildly eccentric a manner. One big yellow fly like a honey-bee comes directly at you with a loud hostile hum or buzz, hovers for a few moments, dashes away in a straight line, turns off at a tangent, and, rushing back again, proceeds with extraordinary velocity to describe curves and circles, parallel lines, angles, and other geometric figures, in the air; and finally drops down within a few inches of you, to remain motionless as a fly carved out of a yellow pebble until the impulse sends him off again. What his motives are, what it all means, we are unable to guess; we can only conclude in our ignorance, judging from appearances, that he is mad. . . . Somewhat of this light-headedness is, I imagine, seen in most of the flies, from the burliest bluebottle to the small gilded variety. What would it be, I wonder, if these minute creatures grew to the size of ducks and geese? Our whole time would be spent in watching their amazing, meaningless antics; nothing else would be talked of or even thought about in the world. In the end, we should become strictly nocturnal, in order to be out of their way, or else we should ourselves go mad in their company.

W. H. Hudson, *Nature in Downland*

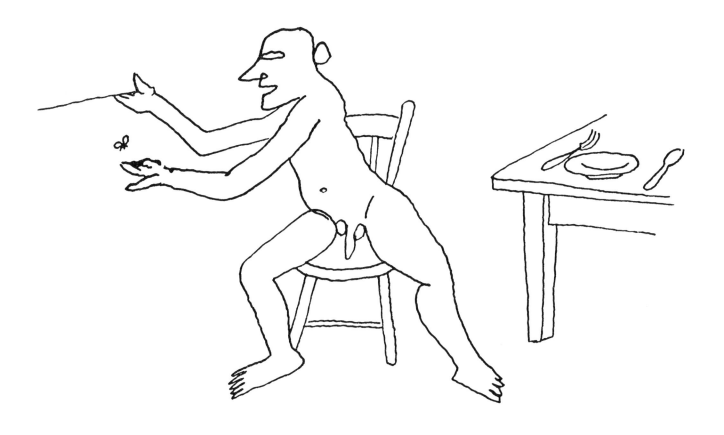

My uncle *Toby* was a man patient of injuries . . . [he] had scarce a heart to retaliate upon a fly.

— Go — says he, one day at dinner, to an over-grown one which had buzzed about his nose, and tormented him cruelly all dinner-time, — and which after infinite attempts, he had caught at last, as it flew by him; — I'll not hurt thee, says my uncle *Toby*, rising from his chair, and going across the room, with the fly in his hand, — I'll not hurt a hair of thy head: — Go, says he, lifting up the sash, and opening his hand as he spoke, to let it escape; — go, poor devil, get thee gone, why should I hurt thee? — This world surely is wide enough to hold both thee and me.

Laurence Sterne, *Tristram Shandy*

THE OWL

Waterton's childhood was spent at Walton Hall, and in his old age he used sometimes to recall the songs of his nurses. "One of them," he said, "is the only poem in which the owl is pitied. She sang it to the tune of 'Cease, rude Boreas, blustering railer,' and the words are affecting: —

'Once I was a monarch's daughter
   And sat on a lady's knee;
But am now a nightly rover,
   Banished to the ivy tree.

'Crying, Hoo, hoo, hoo, hoo, hoo, hoo,
   Hoo, hoo, hoo, my feet are cold!
Pity me, for here you see me
   Persecuted, poor, and old.' "

Norman Moore, *Memoir of Charles Waterton*

Owls have very expressive notes; they hoot in a fine vocal sound, much resembling the *vox humana,* and reducible by a pitch-pipe to a musical key. This note seems to express complacency and rivalry among the males: they use also a quick call and an horrible scream; and can snore and hiss when they mean to menace . . .

A neighbor of mine, who is said to have a nice ear, remarks that the owls about this village hoot in three different keys, in G flat, or F sharp, in B flat and A flat. He heard two hooting to each other, the one in A flat, the other in B flat. *Query:* do these different notes proceed from different species, or only from various individuals? . . .

Gilbert White, *Natural History of Selborne*

There is a singular resemblance between the face of an owl and that of a cat, which is the more notable as both these creatures have much the same kind of habits, live on the same prey, and are evidently representatives of the same idea in their different classes. The owl, in fact, is a winged cat, just as the cat is a furred owl.

J. G. Wood, *Natural History*

Everything in the world is strange and marvellous to well-open eyes. This faculty of wonder is the delight . . . which leads the intellectual man through life in the perpetual ecstasy of the visionary. His special attribute is the wonder of the eyes. Hence it was that the ancients gave Minerva her owl, the bird with ever-dazzled eyes.

José Ortega y Gasset, *Revolt of the Masses*

Tuesday, 8 February 1870

   Miss Child staying at the house again and in great force. She showed me her clever drawings of horses and told me the adventures of the brown wood owl 'Ruth' which she took home from here last year. She wanted to call the owl 'Eve' but Mrs. Bridge said it should be called 'Ruth.' She and her sister stranded in London at night went to London Bridge hotel (having missed the last train) with little money and no luggage except the owl in a basket. The owl hooted all night in spite of their putting her up the chimney, before the looking glass, under the bedclothes, and in a circle of lighted candles which they hoped it would mistake for the sun. The owl went on hooting, upset the basket, got out and flew about the room. The chambermaid almost frightened to death dared not come inside the door. Miss Child asked the waiter to get some mice for 'Ruth' but none could be got.

   Rev. Francis Kilvert, *Diary*

THE EAGLE

He clasps the crag with crooked hands;
Close to the sun in lonely lands,
Ring'd with the azure world, he stands.

The wrinkled sea beneath him crawls;
He watches from his mountain walls,
And like a thunderbolt he falls.

Alfred Tennyson

When thou seest an eagle, thou seest a portion of genius; lift up thy head.

William Blake, *The Marriage of Heaven & Hell*

The Ancients say that the wing-feathers of an *eagle*, mixed with those of common birds, will burn and consume them.

Secrets of Albertus Magnus

For my own part, I wish the bald eagle had not been chosen as the representative of our country; he is a bird of bad moral character; he does not get his living honestly; you may have seen him perched on some dead tree, where, too lazy to fish for himself, he watches the labor of the fishing-hawk; and, when that diligent bird has at length taken a fish, and is bearing it to his nest for the support of his mate and young ones, the bald eagle pursues him, and takes it from him. With all this injustice he is never in good case; like those among men who live by sharping and robbing, he is generally poor, and often very lousy. Besides, he is a rank coward; the little *kingbird*, not bigger than a sparrow, attacks him boldly and drives him out of the district. He is therefore by no means a proper emblem for the brave and honest Cincinnati of America, who have driven all the *kingbirds* from our country; though exactly fit for that order of knights, which the French call *Chevaliers d'Industrie*.

Benjamin Franklin, *Letters*

Dec 21st, 1664. . . . Thence . . . to Mrs. Turner's, in Salisbury Court, and with her a little, and carried her, the porter staying for me, our eagle, which she desired the other day, and we were glad to be rid of her, she fouling our house of office mightily.

Samuel Pepys, *Diary*

MERMAIDS

THE NATURE OF THE SIREN

Strange things indeed   Are seen in the sea-world:
Men say that mermaids   Are like to maidens
In breast and body   But not so below:
From the navel netherward   Nothing looks human,
For there they are fishes   And furnished with fins.
These prodigies dwell   In a perilous passage
Where swirling waters   Swallow men's vessels;
Cheerily they sing   In their changeable voices
That are high and sweet   And hopeful of harm.
This song makes shipmen   Forget their steering
And sink into drowses,   And deeply they dream:
For their vessels are sunken,   Their voyages over.
But wise men and wary   Will turn from these wiles
And often escape   That evil embrace,
Being warned of the mermaids.   Surely this monster,
Half fish and half woman,   Must harbor some meaning.

SIGNIFICATION

Many of mankind   Resemble the mermaid,
Without they wear lambskin,   Within they are wolves;
Their doctrine is righteous,   Their deeds are the Devil's;
Their actions are not   In accord with their utterance;
These two-natured creatures   Will swear by the cross,
By the sun and the moon,   To steer you astray;
With the sweetest of speeches   They swindle their fellows;
They will steal both your substance   And soul with their falsehood.

The Middle English Bestiary

The Mermaide is a sea beast, woonderfully shapen. *Isidore* saith, *Li. II, ca. 3*, where he treateth *De Portentis*, that there be three *Syrenes*, somedeale Maidens, and somedeale foules, with wings & clees. One of them singeth with voice, an other with shamble, and the third with Harpe. Thei please shipmen so greatly with their songe, that they drawe them to peril, and to shipwracke. The cause why they have wings & clees, *Quia Amor & volat, & vulnerat....*

John Bossewell, *Workes of Armorie*

"Do the fishermen along here know anything of the mermaids?" I asked a woman of a village in County Dublin. "Indeed, they don't like to see them at all," she answered, "for they always bring bad weather."

W. B. Yeats, *Irish Fairy and Folk Tales*

These are the seductive voices of the night; the Sirens, too, sang that way. It would be doing them an injustice to think that they wanted to seduce; they knew they had claws and sterile wombs, and they lamented this aloud. They could not help it if their laments sounded so beautiful.

Franz Kafka, *Parables*

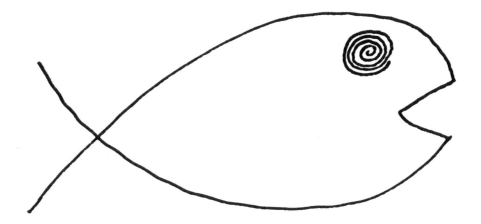

THE FISH

I looked into his eyes
which were far larger than mine
but shallower, and yellowed,
the irises backed and packed
with tarnished tinfoil
seen through the lenses
of old scratched isinglass.
They shifted a little, but not
to return my stare.
— It was more like the tipping
of an object toward the light.

Elizabeth Bishop
from "The Fish"

The fishes in the waters under the earth represent the inhabitants of hell. The waters in Scripture is represented as the place of the dead, the Rephaim, the destroyers; and whales and sea monsters that swim in the great deep are used in Scripture as emblems of devils and the wrath of God, and the miseries of death and God's wrath are there compared to the sea, to the deeps, to floods and billows and the like.

Jonathan Edwards, *Images or Shadows*

Wherefore it befell, on a time when St. Anthony was at Rimini, where was a great multitude of heretics whom he desired to lead to the light of the true faith and to the paths of virtue, that he preached for many days and disputed with them concerning the faith of Christ and of the Holy Scriptures: yet they not only consented not unto his words, but even hardened their hearts and stubbornly refused to hear him. Wherefore St. Anthony, by divine inspiration, went one day to the bank of the river, hard by the seashore, and standing there on the bank of the river, between it and the sea, began to speak to the fishes after the manner of a preacher sent by God, "Hear the word of God, ye fishes of the sea and of the river, since the miscreant heretics scorn to hear it." And when he had thus spoken, anon there came towards the bank such a multitude of fishes, great and small, and middling, that never before in those seas, nor in that river, had so great a multitude been seen; and all held their heads out of the water in great peace and gentleness and perfect order, and remained intent on the lips of St. Anthony: for in front of him and nearest to the bank were the lesser fishes; and beyond them were those of middling size; and then behind, where the water was deepest, were the greater fishes. The fishes being then mustered in such order and array, St. Anthony began to preach to them solemnly, and spake thus: "Ye fishes, my brothers, much are ye held, according to your power, to thank God our Creator, who hath given you so noble an element for your habitation; for at your pleasure have ye waters, sweet and salt, and He hath given you many places of refuge to shelter you from the tempest; He hath likewise given you a pure and clear element, and food whereby you can live. God, your Creator, bountiful and kind, when He created you, commanded you to increase and multiply, and gave you His blessing; then, in the universal deluge and when all other animals were perishing, you alone did God preserve from harm. Moreover, He hath given you fins that ye may fare whithersoever it may please you. To you it was granted, by commandment of God, to preserve Jonah the prophet, and after the third day to cast him forth on dry land, safe and whole. Ye did offer the tribute money to Christ our Lord, to Him, poor little one, that had not wherewithal to pay. Ye, by a rare mystery, were the food of the eternal King, Christ Jesus, before the resurrection and after. For all those things much are ye held to praise and bless God, that hath given you blessings so manifold and so great; yea, more even than to any other of His creatures." At these and the like words and admonitions from St. Anthony, the fishes began to open their mouths and bow their heads, and by these and other tokens of reverence, according to their fashion and power, they gave praise to God. Then St. Anthony, beholding in the fishes such great reverence towards God their Creator, rejoiced in spirit, and said with a loud voice, "Blessed be God eternal, since the fishes in the waters honour Him more than do heretic men; and creatures without reason hear His word better than infidel men."

The Little Flowers of St. Francis

29

THE FOX

THE VIXEN

Among the taller wood with ivy hung,
The old fox plays and dances round her young.
She snuffs and barks if any passes bye
And swings her tail and turns prepared to fly.
The horseman hurries bye, she bolts to see,
And turns agen, from danger never free.
If any stands she runs among the poles
And barks and snaps and drives them in the holes.
The shepherd sees them and the boy goes bye
And gets a stick and progs the hole to try.
They all get still and lie in safety sure
And out agen when everything's secure
And start and snap at blackbirds bouncing bye
To fight and catch the great white butterfly.

John Clare

Having thus far proceeded in our discourse, I cannot think it well done to pass by the cunning of the fox. . . . The mythologists tell us that the dove which Deucalion sent out of his ark, returning back again, was to him a certain sign of the storm not ceased; but of serene and fair weather, when she flew quite away. But the Thracians to this day, when they design to pass a river that is frozen over, make use of a fox to try whether the ice will bear or no. For the fox, treading gently, lays his ears to the ice, and if he perceive by the noise of the water that the stream runs very close underneath, conjecturing from thence that the congelation is not deep but thin, and no way steadfastly solid, he makes a stop, and if he be suffered, returns back again; but if he perceive no noise, he goes on boldly. Nor can we say that this is only an exquisiteness of sense without reason; but it is a syllogistical deduction from sense, concluding that whatever makes a noise is moved; whatever is moved, cannot be frozen; what is not frozen, is moist; what is moist, gives way.

Plutarch, *Water and Land Animals*

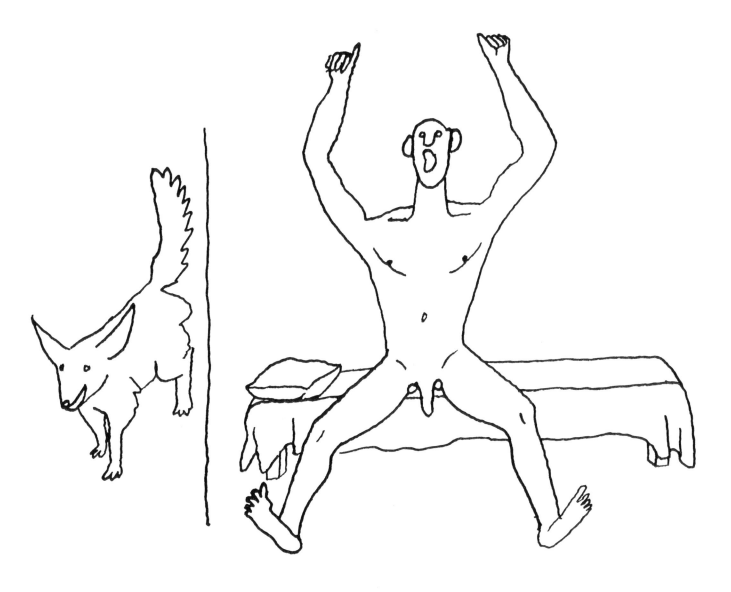

He that will deceive the fox must rise betimes.

George Herbert, *Jacula Prudentum*

Here is the distinct trail of a fox stretching a quarter of a mile across the pond. Now I am curious to know what has determined its graceful curvatures, its greater or less spaces and distinctness, and how surely they were coincident with the fluctuations of some mind, why they now lead me two steps to the right, and then three to the left. If these things are not to be called up and accounted for in the Lamb's Book of Life, I shall set them down for careless accountants. Here was one expression of the divine mind this morning. The pond was his journal, and last night's snow made a *tabula rasa* for him . . .

H. D. Thoreau, *Journals*

THE OSTRICH

from "STRUTHIOCAMELUS"

A wealthy Merchant late in *Barbary*,
Through sandy desarts passing, chanc't to spie
An *Ostrich* eating iron which he found,
By Travellers scattered upon the ground:
Quoth then this Merchant; prithee let me know
What nourishment can from those mettals grow? ...
Thomas Scot

A tame ostrich, or rhea, was kept at the house, and as long as we remained indoors or seated in the verandah he would hang about close by, but would follow us as soon as we started off to the orchard. He was like a pet dog and could not endure to be left alone or in the uncongenial company of other domestic creatures — dogs, cats, fowls, turkeys, and geese. He regarded men and women as the only suitable associates for an ostrich, but was not allowed in the rooms on account of his inconvenient habit of swallowing metal objects such as scissors, spoons, thimbles, bodkins, copper coins, and anything of the kind he could snatch up when no one was looking. In the orchard when he saw us eating peaches he would do the same, and if he couldn't reach high enough to pluck them for himself he would beg of us. It was great fun to give him half a dozen or more at a time, then, when they had been quickly gobbled up, watch their progress as the long row of big round lumps slowly travelled down his neck and disappeared one by one as the peaches passed into his crop.

W. H. Hudson, Far Away and Long Ago

The hunters catch everything with the two or three balls fastened to the thongs of leather; the manner of proceeding is to form themselves into a sort of crescent, each man less than a quarter of a mile apart; one goes some way ahead & endeavours to drive the animals towards the others & thus in a manner encircling them. I saw one most beautiful chase; a fine Ostrich tried to escape; the Gauchos pursued it at a reckless pace, each man whirling the balls round his head; the foremost at last threw them, in an instant the Ostrich rolled over & over, its legs being fairly lashed together by the thong. Its dying struggles were most violent.

Charles Darwin, *The "Beagle" Diary*

HALCYONS

But peacefull was the night
Wherein the Prince of light
   His raign of peace upon the earth began:
The Winds with wonder whist,
Smoothly the waters kist,
   Whispering new joyes to the milde Ocean,
Who now hath quite forgot to rave,
While Birds of Calm sit brooding on the charmed wave.

          John Milton, *On the Morning of Christ's Nativity*

It lays its eggs in the sand hard by the sea, and hatches them in winter when the waves beat hardest against the shore. But the winds all sleep, and the waves are at rest for seven days, while the halcyon sits upon her eggs. And when the young ones come to need their food, then the beneficent God allows seven days more for the growth of this minute creature. And the sailors are aware of this, and call those the halcyon days. And care for the brute creatures is ordained by God, that you may be encouraged to ask of God what you need for your salvation.

          St. Basil, *Hexaemeron*

As to "sea-blue birds" &c. defendant states that he was walking one day in March by a deep-banked brook, and under the leafless bushes he saw the kingfisher flitting or fleeting underneath him, and there came into his head a fragment of an old Greek lyric poet, "ἀλιπόρφυρος ἔιαρος ὄρνις," "The sea-purple or sea-shining bird of Spring," spoken of as the halcyon. Defendant cannot say whether the Greek halcyon be the same as the British kingfisher, but, as he never saw the kingfisher on this particular brook before March, he concludes that in that country, at least, they go down to the sea during the hard weather, and come up again with the Spring, for what says old Belon:

"Le Martinet-pescheur fait sa demeure   Et en esté sur la rivière en estan,
   En temps d'hiver au bord de l'océan,   Et de poisson se repaist à toute heure."

You see he puts "esté," which I suppose stands for all the warmer weather.

          Alfred Tennyson, Letter to the Duke of Argyll

THE WILD BOAR

AUT MORS AUT VITA DECORA

In this our *Emblem*, you shall finde exprest
A *Man*, incountring with a *salvage-beast*;
And, he resolveth, (as his *Motto* sayes)
To *live* with *honour*; or to *dye* with *praise*.
I like the *Resolution*, and the *Deed*,
In which, this *Figure* teacheth to proceed.
For, us, methinkes, it counselleth, to doe
An act, which all men are oblig'd unto.
That ugly *Bore* (wherewith the man in strife
Here seemes to be) doth meane a *Swinish-life*,
And, all those beastly *Vices*, that assay
To root becomming *Vertues* quite away;
Those *Vices*, which not onely marre our features,
But, also, ruinate our manly natures.

George Wither, *Emblemes*

AINEIAS GOES AGAINST IDOMENEUS

He went against Idomeneus, strongly eager for battle,
Yet no fear gripped Idomeneus as if he were a stripling,
but he stood his ground like a mountain wild boar who in the confidence
of his strength stands up to a great rabble of men advancing
upon him in some deserted place, and bristles his back up,
and both his eyes are shining with fire; he grinds his teeth
in his fury to fight off the dogs and the men. So
spear-famed Idomeneus held his ground, and would not give way
to Aineias coming against him . . .

Homer, *Iliad*

Eminent among warlike wild beasts is the Boar. He loves a lair in the farthest depths of the crags and greatly he loathes the noisy din of wild beasts. Unceasingly he roams in pursuit of the female and is greatly excited by the frenzy of desire. On his neck the hair bristles erect, like the crest of a great-plumed helmet. He drops foam upon the ground and gnashes the white hedge of his teeth, panting hotly; and there is much more rage about his mating than modesty. If the female abide his advances, she quenches all his rage and lulls to rest his passion. But if she refuse intercourse and flee, straightway stirred by the hot and fiery goad of desire he either overcomes her and mates with her by force or he attacks her with his jaws and lays her dead in the dust.

There is a tale touching the Wild Boar that his white tusk has within it a secret devouring fiery force. A manifest proof of this for men is well founded. For when a great thronging crowd of hunters with their Dogs lay the beast low upon the ground, overcoming him with long spear on spear, then if one take a thin hair from the neck and approach it to the tusk of the still gasping beast, straightway the hair takes fire and curls up. And on either side of the Dogs themselves, where the fierce tusks of the Swine's jaws have touched them, marks of burning are traced upon the hide.

Oppian, *Cynegetica*

THE ASS

When I must come to you, O my God, I pray
It be some dusty-roaded holiday,
And even as in my travels here below,
I beg to choose by what road I shall go
To Paradise, where the clear stars shine by day.
I'll take my walking-stick and go my way,
And to my friends the donkeys I shall say,
"I am Francis Jammes, and I'm going to Paradise,
For there is no hell in the land of the loving God."
And I'll say to them: "Come, sweet friends of the blue skies,
Poor creatures who with a flap of the ears or a nod
Of the head shake off the buffets, the bees, the flies . . ."

Let me come with these donkeys, Lord, into your land,
These beasts who bow their heads so gently, and stand
With their small feet joined together in a fashion
Utterly gentle, asking your compassion.
I shall arrive, followed by their thousands of ears,
Followed by those with baskets at their flanks,
By those who lug the carts of mountebanks
Or loads of feather-dusters and kitchen-wares,
By those with humps of battered water-cans,
By bottle-shaped she-asses who halt and stumble,
By those tricked out in little pantaloons
To cover their wet, blue galls where flies assemble
In whirling swarms, making a drunken hum.
Dear God, let it be with these donkeys that I come,
And let it be that angels lead us in peace
To leafy streams where cherries tremble in air,
Sleek as the laughing flesh of girls; and there
In that haven of souls let it be that, leaning above
Your divine waters, I shall resemble these donkeys,
Whose humble and sweet poverty will appear
Clear in the clearness of your eternal love.

Francis Jammes

38

There is no character, howsoever good and fine, but it can be destroyed by ridicule, howsoever poor and witless. Observe the ass, for instance: his character is about perfect, he is the choicest spirit among all the humbler animals, yet see what ridicule has brought him to. Instead of feeling complimented when we are called an ass, we are left in doubt.

Mark Twain, *Pudd'nhead Wilson*

THE BEAR

Bears couple in the middle of winter, and not after the fashion of other quadrupeds; for both animals lie down and embrace each other. The female then retires by herself to a separate den, and there brings forth on the thirtieth day, mostly five young ones. When first born, they are shapeless masses of white flesh, a little larger than mice; their claws alone being prominent. The mother then licks them gradually into proper shape . . .

Pliny, *Natural History*

So watchful Bruin forms with plastic care
Each growing lump, and brings it to a Bear.
Alexander Pope, The Dunciad

That a bear brings forth her young informous and unshapen, which she fashioneth after by licking them over, is an opinion not only vulgar, and common with us at present, but hath been of old delivered by ancient writers. Upon this foundation it was an hieroglyphic with the Egyptians; Aristotle seems to countenance it; Solinus, Pliny, and Aelian, directly affirm it, and Ovid smoothly delivereth it;

Nec catulus partu quem reddidit ursa recenti
Sed malè viva caro est, lambendo mater in artus
Ducit, et in formem qualem cupit ipsa reducit.

Which, notwithstanding, is not only repugnant unto the sense of every one that shall enquire into it, but the exact and deliberate experiment of three authentic philosophers. The first, of Matthiolus in his *Comment on Dioscorides* whose words are to this effect: —"In the valley of Anania, about Trent, in a bear which the hunters eventerated or opened, I beheld the young ones with all their parts distinct, and not without shape, as many conceive — giving more credit unto Aristotle and Pliny, than experience and their proper senses." Of the same assurance was Julius Scaliger, in his *Exercitations*. . . . And lastly, Aldrovanus, who from the testimony of his own eyes affirmeth, that in the cabinet of the senate of Bononia, there was preserved in a glass, a cub, taken out of a bear, perfectly formed, and complete in every part.

It is, moreover, injurious unto reason, and much impugneth the course and providence of nature, to conceive a birth should be ordained before there is a formation. . . .

Besides, (what few take notice of,) men hereby do, in a high measure, vilify the works of God, imputing that unto the tongue of a beast, which is the strangest artifice in all the acts of nature. . . .

Sir Thomas Browne, Pseudodoxia Epidemica

THE BEE

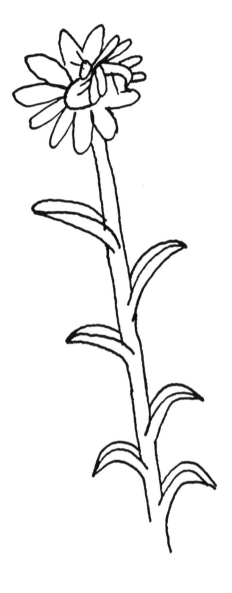

Canterbury. Therefore doth heaven divide
The state of man in divers functions,
Setting endeavour in continual motion;
To which is fixed, as an aim or butt,
Obedience: for so work the honey-bees,
Creatures that by a rule in nature teach
The act of order to a peopled kingdom.
They have a king and officers of sorts;
Where some, like magistrates, correct at home,
Others, like merchants, venture trade abroad,
Others, like soldiers, armed in their stings,
Make boot upon the summer's velvet buds;
Which pillage they with merry march bring home
To the tent-royal of their emperor:
Who, busied in his majesty, surveys
The singing masons building roofs of gold,
The civil citizens kneading up the honey,
The poor mechanic porters crowding in
Their heavy burdens at his narrow gate,
The sad-ey'd justice, with his surly hum,
Delivering o'er to executors pale
The lazy yawning drone.

William Shakespeare, *Henry V*

The bee is more honored than other animals, not because she labors, but because she labors for others.

St. John Chrysostom, *Homilies*

I have described . . . how the Three-horned Osmia, towards the end of her life, when her ovaries are depleted, expends on useless operations such energy as remains to her. Born a worker, she is bored by the inactivity of retirement; her leisure requires an occupation. Having nothing better to do, she sets up partitions; she divides a tunnel into cells that will remain empty; she closes with a thick plug reeds containing nothing. Thus is the little strength of her last hours exhausted in vain work. The other building Bees behave likewise. I see Anthidia laboriously providing numerous bales of cotton to stop galleries wherein never an egg was laid; I see Mason-bees building and then religiously closing cells that will remain unvictualled and uncolonized. . . . The wheels of action go on turning in the absence of the motives for action; they continue their movement as though by a sort of acquired velocity. What clearer proof can we hope to find of the unconsciousness of the animal stimulated by instinct?

J. Henri Fabre, *Bramble-bees and Others*

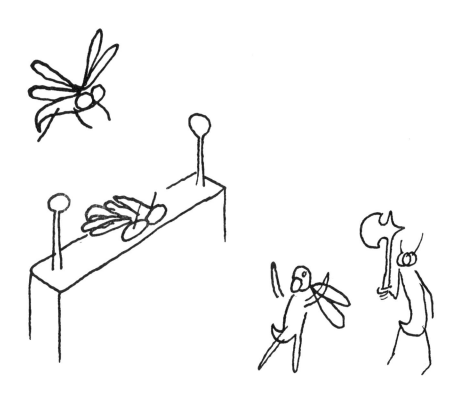

THE PELICAN

PELLICANUS is the word   For a certain breed of bird
Who truly is a crane;   Egypt is his domain.
There are two kinds thereof;   Near to the Nile they live;
One of them dwells in the flood,   The fishes are his food;
The other lives in the isles   On lizards, crocodiles,
Serpents, and stinking creatures,   And beasts of evil nature.
In Greek his title was   *Onocrotalos,*
Which is *longum rostrum,* said   In the Latin tongue instead,
Or *long-beak* in our own.   Of this bird it is known
That when he comes to his young,   They being grown and strong,
And does them kindly things,   And covers them with his wings,
The little birds begin   Fiercely to peck at him;
They tear at him and try   To blind their father's eye.
He falls upon them then   And slays them with great pain,
Then goes away for a spell,   Leaving them where they fell.
On the third day he returns,   And thereupon he mourns,
Feeling so strong a woe   To see the small birds so
Then he strikes his breast with his beak   Until the blood shall leak.
And when the coursing blood   Spatters his lifeless brood,
Such virtue does it have   That once again they live.

KNOW that this pelican   Signifies Mary's Son;
The little birds are men   Restored to life again
From death, by that dear blood   Shed for us by our God.
Now learn one meaning more,   Revealed by holy lore:
Know why the small birds try   To peck their father's eye,
Who turns on them in wrath   And puts them all to death.
Men who deny the light   Would blind God's blazing sight,
But on such people all   His punishment will fall.
This is the meaning I find;   Now bear it well in mind.

Philippe de Thaun, *Bestiary*

Bring the tender tale true of the Pelican;
Bathe me, Jesu Lord, in what thy bosom ran—
Blood that but one drop of has the world to win
All the world forgiveness of its world of sin.

G. M. Hopkins, S. *Thomae Aquinatis*

Of sea foule above all not common in Englande, I noted the Pellicane, which is faigned to be the lovingeste birds that is: which rather then her yong shoulde want, will spare her heart bloud out of her bellie, but for all this lovingness she is very deformed to beholde, for shee is of colour russet, notwithstanding in Guinea I have seene of them as white as a swanne, having legges like the same, and a body like the Herne, with a long necke, and a thicke long beake, from the nether iawe whereof downe to the breast passeth a skinne of such a bignesse, asisable to receive a fishe as bigge as ones thigh, and this her bigge throat and long bill doeth make her seem so ougly.

Sir John Hawkins, *Second Guinea Voyage*

45

THE BUFFALO

THE FLOWER-FED BUFFALOES

The flower-fed buffaloes of the spring
In the days of long ago,
Ranged where the locomotives sing
And the prairie flowers lie low;
The tossing, blooming, perfumed grass
Is swept away by wheat,
Wheels and wheels and wheels spin by
In the spring that still is sweet.
But the flower-fed buffaloes of the spring
Left us long ago.
They gore no more, they bellow no more,
They trundle around the hills no more: —
With the Blackfeet lying low,
With the Pawnees lying low.

Vachel Lindsay

    The buffalo have regular paths by which they come down to drink. Seeing at a glance along which of these his intended victim is moving, the hunter crouches under the bank within fifteen or twenty yards, it may be, of the point where the path enters the river. Here he sits down quietly on the sand. Listening intently, he hears the heavy monotonous tread of the approaching bull. The moment after, he sees a motion among the long weeds and grass just at the spot where the path is channelled through the bank. An enormous black head is thrust out, the horns just visible amid the mass of tangled mane. Half sliding, half plunging, down comes the buffalo upon the river-bed below. He steps out in full sight upon the sands. Just before him a runnel of water is gliding, and he bends his head to drink. You may hear the water as it gurgles down his capacious throat. He raises his head, and the drops trickle from his wet beard. He stands with an air of stupid abstraction, unconscious of the lurking danger. Noiselessly the hunter cocks his rifle. As he sits upon the sand, his knee is raised, and his elbow rests upon it, that he may level his heavy weapon with a steadier aim. The stock is at his shoulder; his eye ranges along the barrel. Still he is in no haste to fire. The bull, with slow deliberation, begins his march over the sands to the other side. He advances his foreleg, and exposes to view a small spot, denuded of hair, just behind the point of his shoulder; upon this the hunter brings the sight of his rifle to bear; lightly and delicately his finger presses the hair-trigger. The spiteful crack of the rifle responds to his touch, and instantly in the middle of the bare spot appears a small red dot. The buffalo shivers; death has overtaken him, he cannot tell from whence; still he does not fall, but walks heavily forward, as if nothing had happened. Yet before he has gone far out upon the sand you see him stop; he totters; his knees bend under him, and his head sinks forward to the ground. Then his whole vast bulk sways to one side; he rolls over on the sand, and dies with a scarcely perceptible struggle.

Francis Parkman, *The Oregon Trail*

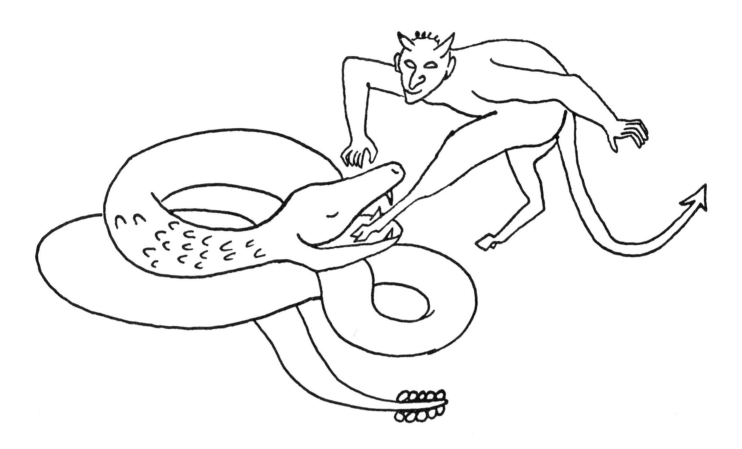

THE
SNAKE

"SATAN ... ENTERS INTO THE
SERPENT SLEEPING"

So saying, through each Thicket Danck or Drie,
Like a black mist low creeping, he held on
His midnight search, where soonest he might finde
The Serpent: him fast sleeping soon he found
In Labyrinth of many a round self rowld,
His head the midst, well stor'd with suttle wiles:
Not yet in horrid Shade or dismal Den,
Not nocent yet, but on the grassie Herbe
Fearless unfeard he slept: in at his Mouth
The Devil enterd, and his brutal sense,
In heart or head, possessing soon inspir'd
With act intelligential; but his sleep
Disturb'd not, waiting close th' approach of Morn.

John Milton, *Paradise Lost*

48

Mr. Darrow. And you believe that is the reason that God made the serpent to go on his belly after he tempted Eve?

Mr. Bryan. I believe the Bible as it is, and I do not permit you to put your language in the place of the language of the Almighty. You read that Bible and ask me questions, and I will answer them. I will not answer your questions in your language.

Mr. Darrow. I will read it to you from the Bible: "And the Lord God said unto the serpent, Because thou hast done this, thou art cursed above all cattle, and above every beast of the field; upon thy belly shalt thou go, and dust shalt thou eat all the days of thy life." Do you think that is why the serpent is compelled to crawl upon its belly?

Mr. Bryan. I believe that.

Mr. Darrow. Have you any idea how the snake went before that time?

Mr. Bryan. No, sir.

Mr. Darrow. Do you know whether he walked on his tail or not?

Mr. Bryan. No, sir. I have no way to know. [Laughter.]

Tennessee v. *Scopes*

All beasts signify affections, . . . and serpents signify the affections of the sensual man, by reason of their creeping on the belly upon the ground in like manner as the sensual principle of man; for this is in the lowest place, and as it were creeps upon the ground under all other principles. . . . The evil . . . who are in the hells, are mostly sensual, and many of them subtle; wherefore when they are viewed from the light of heaven, they appear as serpents of various kinds, and hence it is that the devil is called a serpent.

Emmanuel Swedenborg, *Apocalypse Explained*

Went yesterday to Cambridge and spent most of the day at Mount Auburn; got my luncheon at Fresh Pond, and went back again to the woods. After much wandering and seeing many things, four snakes gliding up and down a hollow for no purpose that I could see — not to eat, not for love, but only gliding. . . .

R. W. Emerson, *Journal*

THE CAT

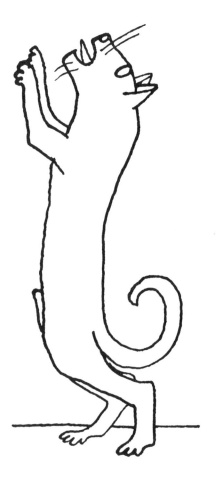

CONCORD CATS

The soft cat and the scratchy cat
Have milk in cold blue plates.
Then, in evenings, star-cool evenings
Equal to their reticence,
Emblems of independence,

These China cats, of black and white,
Will go on planetary pads
Uphill, where crouch
On eighteenth-, seventeenth-century
Houses the graves of Concord.

By pious inscriptions
That antedate the Revolution
They see, through eyes cold and chaste,
The scratchy cat, the soft cat,
With humor old and Oriental,

That nature is meant for poise.
Battles, bloodshed, death,
Are men mirroring time,—
The stars blue, the night paling —
Are data. Imperviousness. Integrity.

Richard Eberhart

Lacenaire, on the same day that he committed a murder, risked his own life to save that of a cat. . . . Wainewright was always very fond of cats; in his last days "his sole companion was a cat for which he evinced an extraordinary affection."

Havelock Ellis, *The Criminal*

Rousseau. Do you like Cats?

Boswell. No.

Rousseau. I was sure of that. It is my test of character. There you have the despotic instinct of men. They do not like cats because the cat is free, and will never consent to become a slave. He will do nothing to your order, as the other animals do.

Boswell. Nor a Chicken, either.

Rousseau. A Chicken would obey your orders if you could make them intelligible to it. But a cat will understand you perfectly, and not obey them.

Boswell. But a Cat is ungrateful and treacherous.

Rousseau. No. That's all untrue. A Cat is an animal that can be very attached to you; he will do anything you please out of friendship. I have a Cat here . . .

James Boswell, *Dialogue with Rousseau*

Inhabits woods of *Europe* and *Asia*: domesticated everywhere; when tranquil purrs, moving the tail; when irritated is very active, climbs, spits, emits a fetid odour; eyes shine at night, the pupil in the day a perpendicular line, by night, large, round; walks with its claws drawn in; drinks sparingly; urine of the male corrosive; breath fetid; buries its excrements; makes a horrid mewling in its amours; mews after and plays with its kittens; wags its tail when looking after prey; the lion of mice, birds, and the smaller quadrupeds; peaceful among its tribe; eats flesh and fish, refuses hot or salted things, and vegetables; washes behind its ears before a storm; back electric in the dark; when thrown up, falls on its feet; is not infested with fleas; gravid 63 days, brings 3-9 young, blind 9 days; delights in marum, cat-mint and valerian.

Carl Linnaeus, *System of Nature*

THE ELEPHANT

FROM "THE SIXTH DAY OF THE FIRST WEEKE"

Of all the Beasts which thou *This-Day* didst build,
To haunt the Hils, the Forrest, and the Field,
I see (as Vice-Roy of their Brutish Band)
The *Elephant*, the vant-guard doth command:
Worthy that office: whether we regard
His Towréd back, where many Souldiers ward;
Or else his Prudence, wherewithall he seems
T' obscure the wits of human-kinde somtimes:
As studious Scholar, he self-rumineth
His lessons giv'n, his King he honoureth,
Adores the Moon: movéd with strange desire
He feels the sweet flames of the *Idalian* fire,
And (pierc't with glance of a kinde-cruell eye)
For humane beauty, seems to sigh and dye.

Guillaume Du Bartas, Divine Weekes

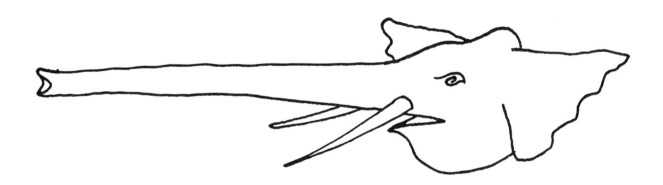

In the amours of animals there is much variety. Some are furious and mad; others observe a kind of human decency, and tricking of themselves to set off their beauty, not without a courtly kind of conversation. Such was the amour of the elephant at Alexandria, that rivalled Aristophanes the grammarian. For they were both in love with a girl that sold garlands; nor was the elephant's courtship less conspicuous than the other's. For as he passed through the fruit-market, he always brought her apples, and stayed with her for some time, and thrusting his proboscis within her waistcoat, instead of a hand, took great delight in gently feeling her breasts.

Plutarch, *Water and Land Animals*

The elephants were some twenty in number. Their drivers, when inducing them to go on board the ships that brought them from Africa to Italy, had promised that they should not be harmed. The promise was not kept. They were exhibited in the Circus on the last day of the shows, and Gaetulians, from Africa, were set to kill them. One animal roused the astonishment of the spectators by fighting on its knees when its feet were wounded, and snatching at its enemies' shields and tossing them in the air, so that they lay round it in a circle, *velut arte non furore beluae iacerentur*. Another was killed by a single javelin that hit it under the eye. But on the whole the exhibition disgusted the spectators. The elephants caused some alarm by trying to break through the iron bars which penned them in. But above all they excited pity by their agonized trumpetings, so that the spectators rose and cursed Pompey for his cruelty. According to Dio, the slaughter had to be broken off; but the elephants which were not killed in the arena were despatched soon afterwards, Pompey having no use for them. Cicero wrote to a friend that the spectacle in the Circus had aroused both pity and a feeling that the elephant was somehow allied with man (*esse quandam illi beluae cum genere humano societatem*).

George Jennison, *Animals for Show and Pleasure in Ancient Rome*

THE GRASSHOPPER

THE GRASSHOPPER

AND THE ANT

Grasshopper, having sung her song
    All summer long,
Was sadly unprovided-for
When the cold winds began to roar:
Not one least bite of grub or fly
Had she remembered to put by.
Therefore she hastened to descant
On famine, to her neighbor Ant,
Begging the loan of a few grains
Of wheat to ease her hunger-pains
Until the winter should be gone.
    "You shall be paid," said she, "upon
My honor as an animal,
Both interest and principal."
The Ant was not disposed to lend:
That liberal vice was not for her.
"What did you do all summer, friend?",
She asked the would-be borrower.
    "So please your worship," answered she,
"I sang and sang both night and day."
"You sang? Indeed, that pleases me.
Then dance the winter-time away."

              Jean de la Fontaine

    The grasshopper alone of this, or any other class of living creatures, has no mouth; but, like those with a caudal sting, it has the appearance of a tongue, long, continuous, and undivided, and with this it feeds upon the dew alone.

              Aristotle, *The History of Animals*

Socrates. A lover of music like yourself ought surely to have heard the story of the grasshoppers, who are said to have been human beings in an age before the Muses. And when the Muses came and song appeared they were ravished with delight; and singing always, never thought of eating and drinking, until at last in their forgetfulness they died. And now they live again in the grasshoppers; and this is the return which the Muses make to them — they neither hunger, nor thirst, but from the hour of their birth are always singing, and never eating or drinking; and when they die they go and inform the Muses in heaven who honors them on earth. They win the love of Terpsichore for the dancers by their report of them; of Erato for the lovers, and of the other Muses for those who do them honor, according to the several ways of honoring them. . . .

Plato, *Phaedrus*

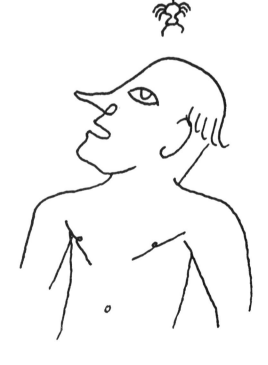

THE SPIDER

A NOISELESS PATIENT SPIDER

A noiseless patient spider,
I mark'd where on a little promontory it stood isolated,
Mark'd how to explore the vacant vast surrounding,
It launch'd forth filament, filament, filament, out of itself,
Ever unreeling them, ever tirelessly speeding them.

And you O my soul where you stand,
Surrounded, detached, in measureless oceans of space,
Ceaselessly musing, venturing, throwing, seeking the spheres
    to connect them,
Till the bridge you will need be form'd, till the ductile
    anchor hold,
Till the gossamer thread you fling catch somewhere, O my soul.
                          Walt Whitman

The only straight line in Nature that I remember is
the spider swinging down from a twig.
                        R. W. Emerson, *Journal*

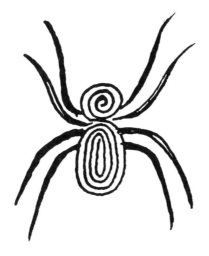

If you will weigh and consider the matter and substance of a Spyders body, you shall find it to be light, pertaking much of fire and ayre, (being two of the most noble and effectall elements in operation) and having but little earthy draggines and drossie refuse. If you behold their figure, they have eyther a Sphaericall and heavenly, or at leastwise an Ovall forme, which is next to the Sphaericall, as beeing the perfectest of all other. Besides, theyr substance is thinne, fine, glystering and subtile, yea although they seeme now and then to be fatted up with plenty of meate, that they grow as bigge in bulke as a Wallnut, and if the learned *Cardan* may be credited, they grow other whiles as great as a Sparrow: yet for all that, if you cast your eye upon them against the light, hanging in their webbe, she glittereth and shineth on all parts like unto the Chrisolite, which is a kind of precious stone, shining with a golden colour quite thorow, causing a pleasant reflection to the eyes, and piercing them with singuler delight.

The colour of a Spyder is some-what pale, such as Ovid ascribeth to Lovers. . . . The skinne of a Spyder is so soft, smooth, exquisite, pure, cleane, and neate, that it farre surpasseth by many degrees, the polished skinnes of those mayds that have the Greenesicknes, or those young whores that are so carefull in sparing no cost to preserve their beauties. . . . Further, it hath fingers, for all the world such as faire virgins desire to have, that is to say, long, round, and slender, beeing also endued with the most exquisite sense of touching that possibly can be imagined. . . .

Thomas Muffet, *Theater of Insects*

REINDEER

"We saw reindeer
browsing," a friend who'd been in Lapland, said:
"finding their own food; they are adapted

to scant *reino*
or pasture, yet they can run eleven
miles in fifty minutes; the feet spread when

the snow is soft,
and act as snow-shoes. They are rigorists
however handsomely cutwork artists

of Lapland and
Siberia elaborate the trace
or saddle-girth with saw-tooth leather lace.

One looked at us
with its firm face part brown, part white, — a queen
of alpine flowers. Santa Claus' reindeer, seen

at last, had gray-
brown fur, with a neck like edelweiss or
lion's foot — *leontopodium* more

exactly." And
this candelabrum-headed ornament
for a place where ornaments are scarce, sent

to Alaska,
was a gift preventing the extinction
of the Esquimo. The battle was won

by a quiet man,
Sheldon Jackson, evangel to that race
whose reprieve he read in the reindeer's face.

Marianne Moore

60

In comparing the advantages which the Laplanders derive from the tame rein-deer, with those which we derive from our domestic animals, we shall see that this animal is worth two or three of them: he is used as horses are, to draw sledges and other carriages; he travels with great speed and swiftness; he easily goes thirty miles a day, and runs with as much certainty upon frozen snow as upon the mossy down. The female affords milk more substantial and more nourishing than that of the cow; the flesh of this animal is very good to eat; his coat makes an excellent fur, and his dressed hide becomes a very supple and very durable leather: thus the rein-deer alone affords all that we derive from the horse, the ox, and the sheep.

Count de Buffon, *Natural History*

THE DEATH OF A TOAD

A toad the power mower caught,
Chewed and clipt of a leg, with a hobbling hop has got
To the garden verge, and sanctuaried him
Under the cineraria leaves, in the shade
Of the ashen heartshaped leaves, in a dim,
Low, and a final glade.

The rare original heartsblood goes,
Spends on the earthen hide, in the folds and wizenings, flows
In the gutters of the banked and staring eyes. He lies
As still as if he would return to stone,
And soundlessly attending, dies
Toward some deep monotone,

Toward misted and ebullient seas
And cooling shores, toward lost Amphibia's emperies.
Day dwindles, drowning, and at length is gone
In the wide and antique eyes, which still appear
To watch, across the castrate lawn,
The haggard daylight steer.

R. W.

THE

TOAD

I remember, Luther pressing men to be thankful, that they are not brought into the lowest condition of creatures, and to bless God that they can see any creature below themselves, gives us a famous instance in the following story: Two *cardinals*, saith he, riding in a great deal of pomp to the council of Constance, by the way they heard a man in the fields, weeping and wailing bitterly; they rode to him, and asked him what he ailed? Perceiving his eye intently fixed upon an ugly toad, he told them that his heart melted with the consideration of this mercy, that God had not made him such a deformed and loathsome creature, though he were formed out of the same clay with it: *Hoc est quod amare fleo*, said he, this is what makes me weep bitterly. Whereupon one of the Cardinals cries out, well, said the Father, the unlearned will rise and take heaven, when we with all our learning shall be thrust into hell.

John Flavel, *Husbandry Spiritualized*

Then Simpleton without more ado went down to the fat toad, and said, "I am to take home the most beautiful woman!" "Oh," answered the toad, "the most beautiful woman! She is not at hand at the moment, but still thou shalt have her." She gave him a yellow turnip which had been hollowed out, to which six mice were harnessed. Then Simpleton said quite mournfully, "What am I to do with that?" The toad answered, "Just put one of my little toads into it." Then he seized one at random out of the circle, and put her into the yellow coach, but hardly was she seated inside it than she turned into a wonderfully beautiful maiden, and the turnip into a coach, and the six mice into horses. So he kissed her, and drove off quickly with the horses, and took her to the King.

Grimm's Fairy Tales

THE UNICORN

I once did see
In my young travels through Armenia,
An angrie Unicorne in his full carier
Charge with too swift a foot a Jeweller,
Who sought him for the Treasure of his browe;
And ere he could get shelter of a tree,
Naile him with his rich Antler to the Earth.

George Chapman, *Bussy D'Ambois*

We were shewn here among other things, the horn of a unicorn, of above eight spans and a half in length, valued at above £10,000.

Paul Hentzner, *Travels in England*

It is sayd that Unicorns above all other creatures, doe reverence Virgines and young Maides, and that many times at the sight of them they growe tame, and come and sleepe beside them, for there is in their nature a certaine savor, wherewithall the Unicornes are allured and delighted: for which occasion the Indian and *Ethiopian* hunters use this stratagem to take the beast. They take a goodly strong and beautifull young man, whom they dresse in the apparrell of a woman, besetting him with divers odoriferous flowers and spices.

The man so adorned, they set in the Mountaines or Woods where the Unicorn haunteth, so as the wind may carrie the savor to the beast, and in the meane season the other hunters hide themselves: the Unicorne deceaved with the outward shape of a woman and sweete smells, commeth unto the young man without feare, and so suffereth his head to bee covered and wrapped within his large sleeves, never stirring but lying still and asleepe, as in his most acceptable repose. Then when the hunters by the signe of the young man perceave him fast and secure, they come uppon him, and by force cut off his horne and send him away alive: but concerning this opinion wee have no elder authoritie then *Tzetzes*, who did not live above five hundred yeares agoe, and therefore I leave the reader to the freedome of his owne judgment, to beleeve or refuse this relation. . . .

Edward Topsell, *Foure-Footed Beastes*

There are wild elephants in the country, and numerous unicorns, which are very nearly as big. They have hair like that of a buffalo, feet like those of an elephant, and a horn in the middle of the forehead, which is black and very thick. They do no mischief, however, with the horn, but with the tongue alone; for this is covered all over with long and strong prickles, and when savage with any one they crush him under their knees and then rasp him with their tongue. The head resembles that of the wild boar, and they carry it ever bent towards the ground. They delight much to abide in mire and mud. 'Tis a passing ugly beast to look upon, and is not the least like that which our stories tell of as being caught in the lap of a virgin; in fact, 'tis altogether different from what we fancied.

Marco Polo, *Concerning the Kingdoms and Marvels of the East*

'A unicorn' is an indefinite description which describes nothing.

Bertrand Russell, *Introduction to Mathematical Philosophy*

THE SHEEP

SHEEP

From where I stand the sheep stand still
As stones against the stony hill.

The stones are gray
And so are they.

And both are weatherworn and round,
Leading the eye back to the ground.

Two mingled flocks —
The sheep, the rocks.

And still no sheep stirs from its place
Or lifts its Babylonian face.

Robert Francis

And, sir, said Christiana, pray let us see some more. So he had them into the slaughter-house, where the butcher was killing a sheep; and, behold, the sheep was quiet, and took her death patiently. Then said the Interpreter, You must learn of this sheep to suffer, and to put up with wrongs without murmurings and complaints. Behold how quietly she takes her death, and without objecting, she suffereth her skin to be pulled over her ears. Your King doth call you his sheep.

John Bunyan, The Pilgrim's Progress

'Why of the sheep do you not learn peace?'
'Because I don't want you to shear my fleece.'

William Blake

Wolves are such furious and mortal enemies of the sheep, that they cherish and maintain that antipathy even after death. For if you bang upon a tambourine fashioned of wolf-skin, in the vicinity of other tambourines fashioned of sheep-skin, these latter will be incapable of a sound — or (as some contend) the skins thereof will burst.

Giovanni Battista Porta, Natural Magic

THE CUCKOO

Repeat that, repeat,
Cuckoo, bird, and open ear wells, heart-springs, delightfully sweet,
With a ballad, with a ballad, a rebound
Off trundled timber and scoops of the hillside ground, hollow
    hollow hollow ground:
The whole landscape flushes on a sudden at a sound.

                         Gerard Manley Hopkins

. . . she doth not build any nest, but layeth her egge in the nest of another, which hatcheth it up as her own . . .

. . . there appears from hence an embleme. For in the Cuckoo is deciphered the wicked practise of adulterous men, who are not ashamed filthily to defile their neighbors bed: From whence we call them cuckolds, who suffer this wrong and yet are innocent . . .

                        John Swan, *Speculum Mundi*

Cuckoo, cuckoo, — O word of fear,
Unpleasing to a married ear!
      William Shakespeare, *Love's Labour's Lost*

This proceeding of the cuckoo, of dropping its eggs as it were by chance, is such a monstrous outrage on maternal affection, one of the first great dictates of nature, and such a violence on instinct, that, had it only been related of a bird in the Brazils, or Peru, it would never have merited our belief.

                  Gilbert White, *Natural History of Selborne*

Many theories, even phrenological theories, have been advanced to explain the origin of the cuckoo laying its eggs in other birds' nests. M. Prévost alone, I think, has thrown light by his observations on this puzzle: he finds that the female cuckoo, which, according to most observers, lays at least from four to six eggs, must pair with the male each time after laying only one or two eggs. Now, if the cuckoo was obliged to sit on her own eggs, she would either have to sit on all together, and therefore leave those first laid so long, that they probably would become addled; or she would have to hatch separately each egg or two eggs, as soon as

laid: but as the cuckoo stays a shorter time in this country than any other migratory bird, she certainly would not have time enough for the successive hatchings. Hence we can perceive in the fact of the cuckoo pairing several times, and laying her eggs at intervals, the cause of her depositing her eggs in other birds' nests, and leaving them to the care of foster-parents.

Charles Darwin, *Journal of Researches*

THE HAWK

Goodyere, I'm glad, and grateful to report
Myself a witness of thy few days' sport;
Where I both learn'd why wise men hawking follow,
And why that bird was sacred to Apollo:
She doth instruct men by her gallant flight
That they to knowledge so should tower upright,
And never stoop but to strike ignorance;
Which if they miss, yet they should re-advance
To former height, and there in circle tarry
Till they be sure to make the fool their quarry.

Ben Jonson

The trained falcon begins to drop like a stone from on high. She falls with the wind whistling through closed wings. Swift as thought she is behind the covey of quail, into it. She misses; up turning she rises. A second time she falls, and as she levels off behind them, her wings whip the air in haste. The covey nears safety in the corn field, but already she is among them. There is a thump, a puff of feathers. She has struck one. Again rising into the air, the falcon turns to flutter down to her fallen prey.

W. F. Russell, Jr., *Falconry*

Standing upon his great rock, Julien beheld the heavens ablaze with August sunlight. Grasshoppers sang in the field below his promontory; whenever their voices grew still, an utter silence surrounded him. He could see twenty leagues of countryside at his feet. From time to time he observed a hawk, which had left the rocky heights above his head, silently describing its vast circles in the air. Julien's eye mechanically pursued the bird of prey. Its calm and powerful movements impressed him; he envied that strength, he envied that isolation.

These things had been Napoleon's destiny; might they not some day be his own?

Stendhal, *The Red and the Black*

Hearing a whole choir of birds chirping and twinkling together, it engaged my curiosity a little to enquire into the occasion of that convocation, which mine eye quickly informed me of, for I perceived a dead hawk in the bush, about which they made such a noise, seeming to triumph at the death of their enemy; and I could not blame them to sing his knell, who, like a cannibal, was wont to feed upon their living bodies, tearing them limb from limb, and scaring them with his frightful appearance. This bird, which living was so formidable, being dead, the poorest wren or titmouse fears not to hop over. This brings to my thoughts the base and ignoble ends of the greatest tyrants, and greedy engrossers of the world, of whom, while living, men were more afraid, than birds of a hawk, but dead, became objects of contempt and scorn. The death of such tyrants is both inglorious and unlamented: *when the wicked perish there is shouting.* Prov. XI. 10. Which was exemplified to the life at the death of Nero, of whom the poet thus sings:

> *Cum mors crudelem rapuisset saeva Neronem,*
> *Credibile est multos Romam agitasse jocos.*
> When cruel Nero dy'd, th' historian tells,
> How Rome did mourn with bonfires, plays and bells.

John Flavel, *Husbandry Spiritualized*

THE WHALE

WHALE is the greatest beast   In all the ocean waste;
Whom if you ever espied   Sprawling upon the tide,
An isle he would seem to be,   Built on the sands of the sea.

When this fierce fish would feed,   He spreads his great mouth wide
And thence expels his breath,   The sweetest smell on earth.
The other fishes come,   Ravished by that perfume;
They dawdle within his jaws,   Unwary of the ruse;
He slams his jaw-gates then,   And drinks those fishes in . . .

This whale-fish dwells secure   Down near the ocean floor
Until that season arrives   When winter with summer strives
And storm stirs all the sea;   In such inclemency
His lair he cannot keep,   But up from the troubled deep
He rises, and lies still.   Then while the weather is ill,
Sailors driven and tossed   Who fear that they are lost,
Sighting the quiet whale,   Mistake him for an isle.
They view him with delight   And hasten with all their might
To make their vessels fast   And climb ashore at last;
With tinder, steel and stone   They kindle a blaze thereon,
Warm them, and drink, and eat.   But, feeling the fire's heat,
The whale to sea-deep dives   And robs them of their lives.

SIGNIFICATION

The Devil is great in will,   With monstrous force and skill
(These powers he imparts   To witches in their arts);
He gives men hunger and thirst   And many another lust,
Drawing them by his breath,   To follow which is death . . .
Who hears the Devil's word   Will rue the day he heard;
Who ties his hopes thereto   Will plunge with him below.

The Middle English Bestiary

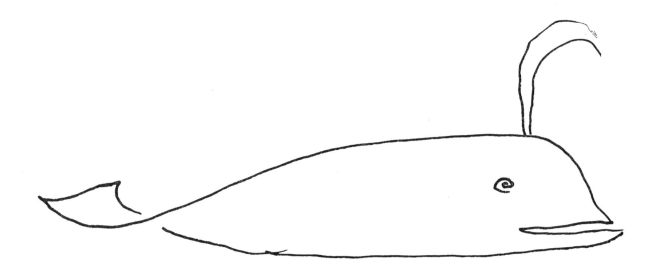

   . . . or that Sea-beast
Leviathan, which God of all his works
Created hugest that swim th' Ocean stream:
Him haply slumbring on the *Norway* foam
The Pilot of some small night-founder'd Skiff,
Deeming some Island, oft, as Sea-men tell,
With fixed Anchor in his skaly rind
Moors by his side under the Lee, while Night
Invests the Sea, and wished Morn delayes:
So stretcht out huge in length the Arch-fiend lay
Chain'd on the burning Lake. . . .

               John Milton, *Paradise Lost*

   . . . this peaking of the whale's flukes is perhaps the grandest sight to be seen in all animated nature. Out of the bottomless profundities the gigantic tail seems spasmodically snatching at the highest heaven. So in dreams, have I seen majestic Satan thrusting forth his tormented colossal claw from the flame Baltic of Hell. But in gazing at such scenes, it is all in all what mood you are in; if in the Dantean, the devils will occur to you; if in that of Isaiah, the archangels. Standing at the masthead of my ship during a sunrise that crimsoned sky and sea, I once saw a large herd of whales in the east, all heading towards the sun, and for a moment vibrating in concert with peaked flukes. As it seemed to me at the time, such a grand embodiment of adoration of the gods was never beheld, even in Persia, the home of the fire worshippers.

               Herman Melville, *Moby Dick*

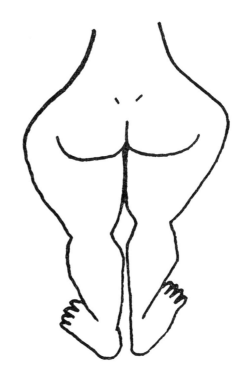

T H E   E N D

Poet, essayist, and translator, RICHARD WILBUR has received the Pulitzer Prize for Poetry, the National Book Award, and a Drama Desk Award, among many other honors. He was named Poet Laureate of the United States in 1987. Wilbur lives in Cummington, Massachusetts.

Known the world over for his signature mobiles and wire sculptures, ALEXANDER CALDER was also a noted illustrator of classic literature. He was awarded a Gold Medal in 1971 by the National Institute of Arts and Letters. Calder died in 1976.